First published in Australia 1988
by Hill of Content Publishing Pty Ltd
86 Bourke Street Melbourne Australia 3000
Copyright© Text: Celeste Sowden
Illustrations: John Forrest
Designed by Jane Wallace-Mitchell
Typeset in Australia by The Composing Room
Printed in Singapore by Kyodo Printing Co Ltd
National Library of Australia
Cataloguing-in-Publication data
Sowden, Celeste.
  Gnome sweet gnome.
  ISBN 0 85572 178 2.
  1. Gnomes – Poetry. I. Forrest, John, 1948-
  II. Title.
A821'.3

Gnome Sweet Gnome

·By Celeste Sowden·
·Illustrated by John Forrest·

HILL OF CONTENT

Dedicated to
Homeless gnomes
or
Gnomeless homes

A personal acknowledgement to Diane Falconer
Who sees beyond the figure... Beyond the form

A Word of Explanation

These whimsical verses sing of garden gnomes; of gnomes who live in a village perhaps a little like yours – who live in the world, but are not of the world.

For theirs is the world of the spirit, the dream and the imagination.

Their actions are dictated by the stars and their conventions by the moon.

They measure time by the turning seasons and success in magical deeds accomplished, yet they echo the human condition, knowing joy and sorrow, laughter and tears.

Some claim that the gnome is the custodian of morality. Others say that the gnome's greatest power is the ability to implant ideas in the minds of men in order to effect change that is positive and productive.

Still others argue that their most important role is the greening of the plants by fortifying magnetic emanation.

What is established is that gnomes hear when we talk to trees, shrubs and flowers, indeed any vegetation.

It's a matter of perception.

For it is common for man to live in a world of practicalities

Where vision is the reality and esoterica a dream

Whereas the gnome lives in the house of magic and make-believe where everything is possible, where the path is the rainbow gold and where the door of promise is always open.

· Max ·
at
Number One

The father of Gnomanic literature
who fashioned the universal motto

'Dare to be gnown'

· Alexander ·
at
Number Two

A victim of mistaken identity.

Day in, day out stands Alexander
upon a rickety verandah
appropriate never for the home
of an aged garden gnome.
To make it worse he cannot move
he's stuck forever in a groove
for he is there to imitate
an aspidistra on a plate.
And no one cares and no one knows
that splinters stick into his toes.

· William ·
at
Number Three

Whose dreams come down to earth.

William stands at No. 3
erect beneath the apple tree
with rosy cheeks and crimson cap
and silver buttons to his lap.
And dreams a dream
and sighs a sigh
for apple blossom days gone by
when pink and white the petals fall
upon the grass and over all
and spill perfume of love's delight
upon the heady wings of night.
So William dreams, through bud and leaf
and grain in golden-laden sheaf.
Then suddenly, for no good reason
(except that it's the proper season)
an apple from a silken thread
descends and clouts him on the head.

· Albert ·
at
Number Four

Who recognizes that stone walls do not a prison
make nor wealth and privilege a kind heart.

Albert lives at No. 4
a mansion with an ivory door
and turrets too, and marble floor
and Persian carpets by the score.
And down the drive sweep limousines
with flashing radar, tinted screens
through wrought iron gates that dogs patrol
and open by remote control.
And at the garage Albert stands
with crimson braid and grey-gloved hands
day in day out from then till now
bent over in a servile bow.
And still he stands a-bending low
whilst sleek Rolls-Royces come and go
deferring yet as their foul soot
paints him black from head to foot.

· Solomon ·
at
Number Five

Who is true to his creed.

Solomon, the wandering gnome
calls anywhere he stands his home
and cogitating on the day
he knows in his wise worldly way
that o'er the world the sky is blue,
a tree is green, the moon is new.
And here or there a gnome could stay
a year, a week, a month, a day
if through a window he could hear
the strains of Mozart sweet and clear.

· Claude ·
at
Number Six

Who sees beyond...

Claude, his eyes fixed on the sky
watches clouds as they float by
and in that vapour on the air
sees every longing painted there.

· Archie ·
at
Number Seven

Who wonders if virtue has its own reward
in the world of men.

Archie, most antique of gnomes
had lost account of all his homes.
But even from a tiny lad
beneath the knee of his old dad
he'd learnt what's meant by being true
efficient, straight and honest too.
He lived his life, no doubts for him
according to this axiom
and steadfastly fulfilled his role
as guardian of a tall flag-pole.
He'd stand erect and to attention
(when people came whose names you mention)
with polished cap and shining face
and watch the flag fly in its place.
He'd watch the flag day in and out
days when there was no one about
in rain and wind and icy gale
he'd guard the flag-pole without fail
and when the sun scorched bricks and stones
he'd stand erect on his old bones
and say, and he believed it too,

"It's good to have a job to do".
And then one bleak and fateful morning
came voices from beneath the awning
as sunshine splashed and dewdrops glistened
Archie braced himself and listened.
"That old dishevelled heap of clay
must be tossed out this very day
he's ugly, chipped, look at his leg
hardly straighter than a peg.
Old things must go, bring in the new
that's what I intend to do."
"But dear, my dear..." old Archie heard
"Let me have just one small word.
This gnome's been faithful, ever true
and even if he isn't new,
a coat of paint, a bit of plaster
would help..." she started to speak faster.
"No, no, I will not hear it. No.
He's old and ugly, has to go.
He's past it, way beyond his prime
he's useless now, he's had his time."
"He's done his job and done it well."
"No madam, he can go to hell!"
(Thinks he, 'I'll find a way to suit her,
I'll have one trained as a computer').
So Archie most antique of gnomes
who'd lived in oh so many homes,
was tossed upon a pile of stones

that broke his heart and broke his bones
and as he settled down to die
he gave this last sad little cry
"Though tarnished, chipped and most forlorn
I did not warrant such cruel scorn
and that young modern gnome will he
do the job as well as me?"

· Harold ·
at
Number Eight

A lover of things beautiful.

Harold in petalled earth-bed knows
of all that in the garden grows
of all that man in homage sows
the loveliest ever is the Rose.

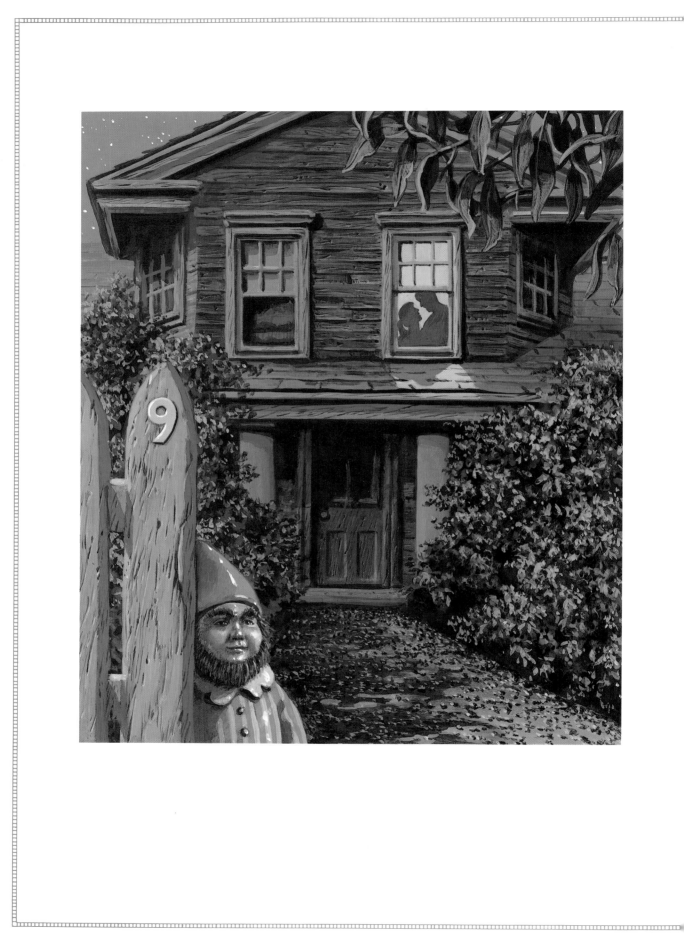

· Henry ·
at
Number Nine

*Who laments his unrequited love
for the mistress of the house.*

Will milady come again?
The earth is still: I wait in vain
for fragrance, diffused in the air
for silver laughter trembling there
for gracious form, for angel face
an air as delicate as lace.
Oh gentle dryad of the night
with orbs a-sparkling diamond bright
you are my secret fairy queen
in palace set in woodland green.
You're lovelier more than I can say
sweeter than any summer's day
and every dream and every plan
would be for you, were I a man.

· Edward ·
at
Number Ten

Who admits that sometimes
even gnomes grumble.

When after gentle springtime showers
and tiny buds burst into flowers
Edward sighs and asks anew,
"Why oh why can't I grow too?"

· Alfonso ·
at
Number Eleven

Whose allergies prompted
a universal movement.

Alfonso was not hard to please
yet he complained of allergies.
The trouble started with his breathing
noxious gases round him wreathing.
Soon he was inflamed and wheezing
sneezing, sneezing, sneezing, sneezing.
His garden stood so close to where
thick smoke from chimneys filled the air
factories having much to do
with cranes and drills and ladders too
where workmen on the topmost rungs
inhaled the filth into their lungs.
"Those men will die before their time,"
thought Alf, 'This is indeed a crime.
The smoke that billows in the air
and waste should be expelled elsewhere:
it should be buried underground
a method that is much more sound.'
Alfonso then posed this solution
to rid the air of foul pollution
a common practice now we see
thanks to Alfonso's allergy.

· Simeon ·
at
Number Twelve

Who abides in faith, hope, love.

Simeon, his leg of plaster
shattered by a drunken master
was tossed into the garden shed
his broken leg flung at his head
and in foul fertiliser haze
he staggers out his nights and days.
But from the dark slime-smelling floor
he sees the light beneath the door.

· Fred ·
at
Number Thirteen

Who smiles in the face of discomfort.

Fred always smiles, a happy fellow
with hat of green and coat of yellow
and watches dogs of every hue
anticipating what they'll do.

· Fiori ·
at
Number Fourteen

Whose philosophy might be heeded.

An aged gnome, by name Fiori
recounted this unhappy story
whilst in a garden overgrown
with tangled weeds and vines self-sown
and stunted trees – for in this plight
they hardly ever glimpsed the light.
"But", said Fiori, "Long ago
some twenty seven years or so
life was a joy; the timbers rang
with children's voices as they sang
and played and laughed from dusk till dawn
about the house and on the lawn
(the lawn those days you should have seen
it looked just like a bowling green).
The house belonged to Mr. Brown
an engineer who worked in town
a man respected in his work
for complex task he'd never shirk.
Miss Bott would meet him at the door
(his wife had died two years before)
she kept the house and cooked and sewed
she made sure that the lawns were mowed

and tried to curb his three young girls
with willow waists and golden curls
who as they grew proved plainly spoiled
especially if their plans were foiled.
Well time went by and Mr. Brown
lost his respected job in town.
One rainy night he came home drenched
to say that he had been retrenched
and sadly showed Miss Bott the door
'I can't afford you anymore'.
The girls, alert to his state fully
married men whom they could bully.
No skill, profession, job or rank
but lots of money in the bank.
'The old man's no use now, he's broke.
It won't be long before he'll croak.
His cheque account is showing nil.
It's not worthwhile to read the will'.
Things of value each one took
and left without a backward look.
Mr. Brown grew ill and weak
with sunken eye and pallid cheek
upon his grimy counterpane
a throbbing ache inside his brain
and no one came and on the ground
the weeds and nettles grew around
and where there once were flower beds
tangled thistles raised their heads.

Mr. Brown lay on his bed
'I think I'm very nearly dead
I know now and it's almost funny
they only loved me for my money'.
He died, an end to jibes and mocks
and went out carried in a box.
His daughters came back to the place
'Just look at it, it's a disgrace
it's so neglected, so run down
the most ramshackle house in town.' "

Fiori sighed and said, "My friend
my tale is nearly at an end
all's wasteland now as you can see
the only thing alive is me.
But I will stay here to commend
that men, like gardens one must tend
for when they wild and careless grow
it's too late then to start to mow."

· George ·
at
Number Fifteen

Who would be emblazoned
in sartorial splendour.

George's clothes are dull and faded
and when he's grumpy, glum or jaded
he asks himself, "Why is it that
the birds must sit upon my hat?"

· Arthur ·
at
Number Sixteen

Who remained true to his stolid disposition.

Arthur, uncomplaining chap
stands silently beneath a tap
which drips all day, his paint defacing
because the washer needs replacing.
And with the wetness all around
young Arthur's sinking underground
all you can witness is his hat
and very little now of that.
"Oh dear," said Arthur, speaking low
"I haven't very far to go.
Had I complained of my sad plight
I'd be above the ground upright.
A time to speak, a time to bow –
in any case, it's too late now."

· Horace ·
at
Number Seventeen

Who realises that retaliation
is not the answer.

"Yes", thinks Horace, "to be stoic
is better than to be heroic"
as the spider, spinning near
hooks her web on to his ear.

· Cedric ·
at
Number Eighteen

Who achieved world acclamation
and won the Gnobel prize
for the famed Bignomial Theorem,
a mathematical treatise.

· Herbert ·
at
Number Nineteen

Shamed because of a proboscis.

Herbert's nose
was of the size
to warrant winning
a first prize.
Red, round and fiery
like a funnel
and nostrils wider
than a tunnel.
'Twas quite unique
our Herbert's beak.
But sad it is to tell
that this gnome's shame
just grows and grows
because his nose
supports the hose.

· Guido ·
at
Number Twenty

Who tends to think that ignorance is bliss.

Guido in recumbent pose
decked in gaily painted clothes
watches knees and legs and feet
about the garden in the street
feet that shuffle, run and skip
kick and stamp or lightly trip.
"I know my feet," he said, "I think
those terra cotta bricks of pink
hide many dispositions too
the gait of leg is the first clue.
The garden stork from his high place
might, if I asked, describe each face."

The stork bent low to Guido's ear
and what he said one couldn't hear.
But Guido smiled, "Your detail's neat
I think I'll stick to watching feet."

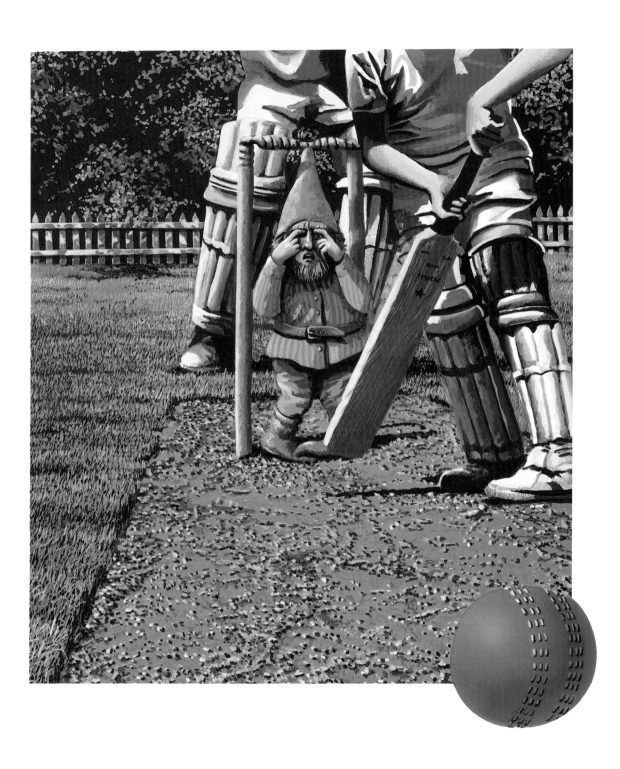

· Stanley ·
at
Number Twenty One

Who would spend the twilight
at peace and in reflection.

Long summer evenings on the grass
that's soft and springy as you pass
each blade is close-clipped and the reason
is the coming cricket season.
Oh then obserye poor Stanley quake
and see his legs begin to shake.
This strange behaviour comments Stanley
is hardly gnoble, hardly manly.
But how would you react, when boys
with bats and balls, with raucous noise
arrive to play a game of cricket
and use you for the blinking wicket?

· Patrick ·
at
Number Twenty Two

Who knows that where there's a will
there's a way.

Seven Oaks is Patrick's home
next door there lives a lady gnome
and though they're neighbours in the street
they know that they will never meet
for each year past and each year hence
they're separated by a fence.
And Patrick in his reverie
sees pale pink hat and stockinged knee
and thinks if he could make connection
she might respond to his affection.
But ever yet love conquers all
and through the oak tree branches tall
on fragile wings unto his queen
the sweetheart whom he's never seen
come perfumed notes and tender words
delivered by some friendly birds.

· Bernard ·
at
Number Twenty Three

Who concentrates for a purpose.

Bernard thinks on love and care
of a world we all may share
he fixes his ideas and then
transfers them to the minds of men.

· Humphrey ·
at
Number Twenty Four

Who thinks that if people have gardens
they should tend them.

Humphrey's peeved, he's angry, riled
for in his garden, growing wild
the pampas grass and black bamboo
eclipse his tiny frame from view.
And with more growth, I do declare
he'll need a snorkel for fresh air.

· Thomas ·
at
The Vicarage

– an apostolic gnome.

Thomas says a little prayer
as night's soft curtain closes round
the trees and houses everywhere
and paints its blackness on the ground.
And then, when everything is still
when party-goers have tip-toed in
and when the hearth is cold and chill
and wood-logs stacked inside the bin

Thomas says, "Put out the light
It's time to wish the world good-night."